S0-AXY-618

IMPRESSIONS IN CLAY

IMPRESSIONS IN CLAY

Learning to Live Under the Master's Hand

WENDY LAWTON

MOODY
PUBLISHERS

CHICAGO

© 2005 by
WENDY LAWTON

All rights reserved. No part of this book may be reproduced in any form without permission in writing from the publisher, except in the case of brief quotations embodied in critical articles or reviews.

Scripture quotations, unless otherwise indicated, are taken from the *Holy Bible, New International Version*®. NIV®. Copyright © 1973, 1978, 1984 by International Bible Society. Used by permission of Zondervan Publishing House. All rights reserved.

Scripture quotations marked KJV are from the King James Version.

Interior design: www.DesignByJulia
Pottery images: ©2005 JupiterImages Corporation
Illustrations: JoAnn Anderson

Library of Congress Cataloging-in-Publication Data
Lawton, Wendy.
Impressions in clay : learning to live under the Master's hand / Wendy Lawton.
    p. cm.
  ISBN-10: 0-8024-1502-4
  ISBN-13: 978-0-8024-1502-8
  1. Spirituality. 2. Spiritual life--Christianity. 3. Clay--Miscellanea.
I. Title.
  BV4501.3.L398 2005
  248.4--dc22
            2005021656

1   3   5   7   9   10   8   6   4   2

Printed in the United States of America

FOR BETTY RODRIQUEZ

Who helped me learn to

savor the mystery of our faith

and discover the power

of simple prayer

CONTENTS

POEM: The Uncontainable

Acknowledgments

Special thanks to the twelve who partnered with me in prayer for this book—Kris Metcalf, Kathy Nyman, Mary Wickstrom, Dorothy De Sa, Betty Doine, Dan Johnson, Penny Forgnone, Debby Lundell, Elvira Englund, Mavis Kronberg, Olive Lindquist, and Kim Lonjin.

And to my husband, Keith, who's encouraged my pursuits for close to thirty-five years—messy ones like clay, paint, and porcelain, and time-consuming ones like writing, speaking, and teaching.

My three children continue to teach me about the Potter's handiwork as I watch their emerging vessels.

I'm indebted to JoAnn Anderson for her sensitive pencil illustrations of the Potter and clay. JoAnn and I have worked together for many years, and her skill and vision have only deepened with time.

I appreciate the wise words of the writers quoted within the text, especially my friend, Marlene Chase, editor in chief and literary secretary for The Salvation Army in the United States, who wrote the poems *The Master Potter* and *The Uncontainable* for this book.

And, as always, I'm beholden to the incomparable editorial and design team at Moody Publishers—especially my editor, Peg Short, who caught the vision and helped me transform the clay of my ideas into a usable vessel—and to my friend and agent, Janet Grant.

THE MASTER POTTER

He moves amid the potsherds,
with patient, practiced eye
saves fragments of divinity
shattered by outrageous winds.
Plying His grand, inscrutable trade,
He grinds yet more the useless shards
and kneads them into clay.
Defying gravity, years and tears,
He spins on shaft and wheel
this chaos of broken hopes.
With wounded fingers, flamed by love,
He sculpts a form of tensile grace
and fills it with Himself.

MARLENE CHASE

TRANSFORMING CLAY

"Like clay in the hand of the potter,

so are you in my hand."

JEREMIAH 18:6

*"Woe to him who
quarrels with his
Maker, to him who is
but a potsherd among
the potsherds on the
ground. Does the
clay say to the potter,
'What are you making?'
Does your work say,
'He has no hands'?"*

(ISAIAH 45:9)

Clay.

It's not the most glamorous substance, yet throughout the Bible, God uses clay to teach us about ourselves. When I told a friend I planned to write about the Potter and clay she asked, "How in the world can you say anything new about that timeworn metaphor?"

It's a fair question. We're all familiar with the imagery of God as the Potter and us as the clay, but how might a sculptor, who understands the intricate, multi-step process of creating with clay, understand that metaphor?

I'll never forget the first time I picked up a lump of clay. A brave kindergarten teacher introduced us to ceramics by lugging a twenty-five-pound bag of clay into the classroom. After dividing it up, she showed us how to roll snaky coils of clay and wind them into a pot of sorts. I had decided to make an egg dish for my little sister, so mine was only about two coils high. I had no idea how this squishy stuff would ever be a plate, but from my limited experience, kindergarten held many mysteries. This ceramic project couldn't be any more amazing than discovering that squiggly lines of writing could be separated into words.

Once I smeared the coils into a semblance of smoothness, I took a pencil eraser and dotted deep crevices onto the entire surface. But we weren't done. Several days later, our teacher handed us back our dry, chalky objets d'art along with a soft flat paintbrush. We picked our colors from a chart. The teacher gave me a jar of milky glaze that looked nothing like the color

I'd chosen. Our roomful of five-year-olds slopped glaze onto the clay with abandon. The whole project was a lesson in faith—the egg dish I eventually took home was a shiny pink. That day I became a believer in the mystery of clay.

One of the most vivid biblical passages about clay comes when the Lord gave Jeremiah an assignment: "Go down to the potter's house, and there I will give you my message" (Jeremiah 18:2). Jeremiah tied on his sandals and hurried to obey. God had commissioned the prophet as a youth, and in all that time he had never questioned his undertaking. He knew from experience that the Lord often revealed Himself in unexpected ways.

Imagine as he made his way through the City of David—the dust from the road must have coated his feet and collected in the coarse fibers of his garment. Jeremiah saw the mounds of raw clay as he drew near the pottery sheds. Pottery was a major industry in Jerusalem during

Jeremiah's day, and the potteries were located in settlements in the lower city, near the rich clay deposits in the Valley of Hinnom. Before long, the prophet could smell the earthy fragrance of damp clay and feel the heat of the simple outdoor kiln.

Jeremiah lowered his head to enter the potter's house. The craftsman barely looked up as he rhythmically treadled his wheel. The potter's wheel consisted of two parallel stone or clay wheels connected by a shaft. As the potter moved the lower wheel with his bare feet, the upper wheel rotated smoothly. A vessel of water sat nearby to sluice the clay, keeping it moist and pliable.

Jeremiah watched the potter's skillful hands encircle the rotating lump of clay to center it. As the clay became perfectly centered on the moving wheel, the potter pressed his thumbs deep into the center of the clay to begin the process of opening it. Once opened into a bowl-like form, he expanded the shape upward by applying pressure with his inside fingers against his outside fingers. As the pot grew, Jeremiah could see that it wobbled on the wheel. Seeing that it was off balance, the potter let out his breath. With the wheel still moving, his hands pressed the flawed vessel back into a lump of wet clay.

We've lost familiarity with this craft over the centuries. The materials are as much a mystery to us as the process of ceramics and the work of the potter—but not to Jeremiah. The potter was a familiar fixture in Jeremiah's world. The prophet stood that day on the dusty floor of the potter's workshop and watched the subtleties of God's message unfold before his eyes. He knew the process, the smells, the sounds, and the cool smoothness of a hand-thrown clay pot. As the wheel turned and clay slip spattered his sandals, Jeremiah silently observed the potter and connected the process to God's plans and to deep spiritual truths. He understood.

As a professional sculptor, this image of potter and clay speaks volumes to me. Long after my kindergarten experience with the pink egg plate, clay reentered my life. In fact, over the last twenty-five years. I've been intimately acquainted with clay. I've felt the coolness of a lump of clay in my hand. I recognize the earthy smell. I've even tasted the chalkiness as I moisten a tiny ball of clay in my mouth. I don't make the useful vessels akin to Jeremiah's potter, nor do I use a potter's wheel—but I can't help marveling at this rich metaphor God gave us.

Through the pages of this book, we'll examine how the potter mines the clay, common dirt from the ground. We'll see him slab the clay with great force to make it elastic and flexible. We'll watch him throwing the pot, a process that requires a balance of pressure and movement, sluiced with water. As we watch, he'll squash down the pot many times during the process. After the pot is formed, the potter will set the vessel aside to dry before he coats it with a dull glaze. The pot, at this stage, may look finished; but if water were poured into it, it would melt back into mud. The mystery happens after the intense heat of the kiln. A metamorphosis occurs. The glaze has turned a beautiful crystalline color.

But—so what?—you might say.

When we stop to unwind the meaning of the metaphor, there are many lessons for us in the process. Like how often we rise off the Potter's wheel, only to be thumped back down again. Or how we sometimes decide we've come far enough to be able to hold water, only to melt into a shapeless lump of clay again because we haven't spent enough time in the fire. And what about the dull coat of frit that we see in the mirror each day? Someday it may actually be a crystalline color so pure and beautiful that it will reflect the face of the Potter in the surface.

I admit it. It can be dangerous to push a metaphor beyond its illustrative purpose. C. S. Lewis said,

"A symbol has a life of its own. An escaped metaphor—escaped from the control of the total poem or philosophy in which it belongs—may be a poisonous thing." Our metaphor, however, is not a single escaped metaphor. The Bible is filled with potter-and-clay imagery—the Potter nearly always refers to God and the clay to His people. Because it's a recurring theme, it begs to be explored. We probe for further lessons from the transformation of raw earth like Jeremiah observed in the potter's house. We long to experience the transforming power of God in our lives—and by carefully observing the artist, truths about the process of transformation emerge.

As we dig deeper, we'll investigate the ceramic process and consider some of the spiritual lessons. The beauty of a metaphor, however, is that the meaning unwinds uniquely for each seeker. By understanding the process of creating a work of art, each of us may uncover our own applications.

Taking Jeremiah 18:1–6 literally, we see that the Lord was giving His prophet a specific message for the house of Israel. It was simple: God is in control. He can raise the nation up just as the potter raised the clay, or He can thump it back down. The hoped-for response was equally simple: The Lord called for the nation to repent and acknowledge His sovereignty. The consequence for ignoring the call to repentance and continuing Israel's morbid fascination with idolatry was clear—God would destroy the unrepentant nation. The warning itself bore a familiar ring. Isaiah had issued a similar admonishment a little more than a century earlier. "Woe to him who quarrels with his Maker, to him who is but a potsherd among the potsherds on the ground. Does the clay say to the potter, 'What are you making?' Does your work say, 'He has no hands'?" (Isaiah 45:9).

The object lesson at the potter's house made the point with chilling eloquence. Jeremiah knew what he must say to the people.

And, beyond the literal account, this picture of the potter and clay is a story of becoming, a story of transformation. Throughout the lessons in this book, we'll savor the images, dust off revealing details obscured by time, and uncover what it feels like to be clay in the Potter's hands.

I AM WORTHY

W

"God gives us his light in an instant, allowing us to know all we need to know. No more is necessary in his plan to lead us to perfection. We cannot seek this light; it is given to us from God only as he chooses. Neither do we know how it comes, or how we even know that it is! If we try to know more than we have been made to know, we will accomplish nothing. We simply wait like a stone until he brings us to life."

CATHERINE OF GENOA (1447–1510)

I Am Worthy Because He Chose Me

"You did not choose me, but I chose you."

JOHN 15:16

When I first began to work with clay, I quickly learned that the success of the end product depended on the raw materials chosen. In the same way, much of the beauty of the final jar and the success in forming it are due to the properties of the raw clay. Jeremiah's potter didn't have the luxury of lugging home a twenty-five-pound bag of commercially prepared earthenware clay, fully wedged and ready to be worked. He quarried his own clay. Great care must have gone into the choosing. Perhaps the potter spent a hot, dirty morning digging deeply into clay deposits in a promising spot, only to finally judge the clay overly crumbly and unsuitable for throwing.

In my own work as a doll sculptor, I cast with porcelain slip made of kaolin clays from Europe. Porcelain is considered the ultimate clay—more translucent and refined than any other. I'm fortunate to live in a day when I don't have to mine my own clays and create my own slip. Clay companies have geologists and artists who specialize in the development of fine clay. As a sculptor, I know that to create a face that seems to glow from within, I need to choose the clay carefully. Over the years I've tested and rejected dozens of clays—too chalky, too dull, too heavy. It takes a far more skillful artist than I to take inferior clay and coax near perfection out of it.

I imagine that day Jeremiah visited the potter's shed, he missed seeing the potter quarry the clay, but that was nonetheless an important part of the process. Days before Jeremiah's visit, the potter may have taken his handcart out through the Potsherd Gate to the rich terra-cotta clay deposits in the valley.

REFLECTIONS

"I believe the doctrine of election because I am quite sure that if God had not chosen me, I never would have chosen Him; and I am sure He chose me before I was born or else He never would have chosen me afterwards."

CHARLES SPURGEON
1834–1892

Clay comes from the decomposition of igneous feldspar, the most common element of the earth's crust. It's formed from the cooling of molten magma thrust up from deep inside the core. Jeremiah's potter may not have known that his clay was made up of two minerals—alumina and silica—but he knew well how to judge its suitability for his vessels.

When the potter dug into the clay bed, he probably reached down and took a handful to gauge the plasticity of the raw material. Surface clay is usually mixed with too much extraneous matter—humus, soil, roots, and rock. Over the centuries the potter would have stuck with a rich vein and quarried deeper and deeper into the clay deposit. He would have known a good clay must be flexible enough to be thrown without sagging and to join without cracking, but few clays are perfect as found. If the clay is too plastic (too soft to hold shape), the potter will add grog (ground particles of broken pottery) to increase strength.

Our lives are much like the interior clay—filled with imperfections. Yet we are the clay that the Master Potter has chosen. And He is the One who provides the strength and flexibility to the clay. When He sees the sag, He adds grog. When the clay gets too dry, He adds water. What a lesson for us. The Potter is not only in control of the process of forming us, He controls our raw material as well. We need only reach out for His strength and His living water.

We see a powerful spiritual application in the potter's act of choosing the clay. The potter saw the potential beauty of the imperfect clay. When I take time to contemplate the mystery of the Potter scooping up my claylike self and choosing me for His work in progress, it always begs the question—why me?

The honor bestowed mystifies us. It's like my very first week in kindergarten at Hawthorne Elementary School in San Francisco. The doors were way too big and way too heavy to open, and I worried about getting shut out or locked in. Scary. I'd never seen so many children together in one room, but the teacher gave us real scissors and delicious-tasting paste. And, best of all, in the middle of discovering all these wonders, my teacher picked me to be milk monitor. Out of all those other children, she picked me! I never forgot that honor, and it colored my whole educational career.

The psalmist takes us there in Psalm 8:4: "What is man that you are mindful of him, the son of man that you care for him?"

In wonder we ask, "Why me?" And it takes a lifetime to absorb the answer. When we begin to grasp the truth, it comes with a Sally Field–like sense of discovery: "You like me. You really like me."

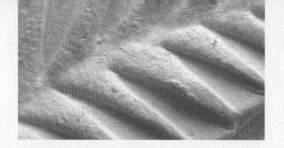

F ather, You formed us from the dust of the earth and gave us the illustration of clay in the potter's hand. Help us remember that Your Potter's hand scooped that fistful of dust off the earth and made the clay for Your vessels. How we get things backward. Too often we talk about choosing You—as if the clay chooses the Potter. Forgive us, Lord. Amen.

I Am Stronger

I AM STRONGER

S

"God has a unique way of scooping up the
shattered fragments of our hopes and dreams
and molding them into a plan of his own
—a plan vastly different from ours,
but far more wonderful."

ANITA DITTMAN, HOLOCAUST SURVIVOR (1927–TODAY)

I AM STRONGER BECAUSE OF BROKENNESS

"I am like a broken vessel."

PSALM 31:12 KJV

Our farmhouse is the oldest home in our area. It sits on a thirty-acre almond farm in the country. In the early part of the last century, instead of having trash pickup like today, the farmer would dig a deep hole into which the family would throw garbage. When the pit filled up, he covered it over and dug a new dumpsite. These long-buried refuse repositories dot our property. In time everything decomposed or rusted away except glass and bits of pottery. Now, when I garden, I often turn over a shovelful of dirt only to find a shard of a willowware plate or a piece of a flow blue teacup.

In Jerusalem, around the Potsherd Gate, they didn't bother to bury their trash. Broken pieces of pottery littered the ground for as far as the eye could see. It's no wonder. Loss is inherent in the craft, no matter how skillful the potter. He loses a portion of each firing—some from firing defects, kiln cracks, or trapped air; others because of weaknesses inherent in the clay body. No craftsman wants to risk having inferior work make its way into the marketplace, so as soon as a defective pot cooled, he would smash it, eventually carting the broken pieces out to the pottery dump of their day—the area outside the Potsherd Gate.

Further on in the Jeremiah passage, God tells the prophet to go back to the potter's house, this time as a customer. God instructed Jeremiah to buy a fired clay jar and take it out to the Potsherd Gate. The prophet was to call the people together, and after he told the crowd what God revealed in the potter's house, he was to break the jar and say, "This is what the LORD Almighty says: I will smash this nation and this city just as this potter's jar is smashed and cannot be repaired" (Jeremiah 19:11). Jeremiah had his assignment.

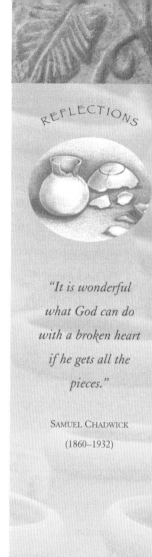

REFLECTIONS

"It is wonderful what God can do with a broken heart if he gets all the pieces."

SAMUEL CHADWICK
(1860–1932)

As Jeremiah carried the jar out to the gate, the people must have wondered what kind of tirade the prophet planned to deliver this time. He was far from popular because he spoke the messages of condemnation exactly as they came from the Lord—no mincing words or trying to make the message palatable to the masses. The people followed and listened to his words. They couldn't help themselves. Who knows if curiosity or something else drew the crowds. While they knew about prophets sent from God, they still managed to dismiss His warnings.

But Jeremiah delivered a powerful sensory message that day. Perhaps as he smashed the jar against the gate, the sound reverberated through the valley, punctuated by gasps from the crowd. The fragments of the pot flew, adding to the potsherd debris, possibly causing a ripple of movement through the crowd as those in front pushed back to avoid the shower of shattered pieces. As the people turned back toward the city, they must have moved gingerly through the rubble, crunching potsherds underfoot.

The prophet had given them an unforgettable illustration of his warning. Would the smashed nation of Israel look like that potter's field, littered with brokenness?

Like Jeremiah's potter, God can make a pot (or a nation), destroy it, and then make a new one of reconstituted material. Or He can take a seemingly functional vessel and smash it. He can make a new covenant to replace the old. This lesson to the hardened house of Israel is sobering. God would need to shatter them and their pride before they could be made new.

But all is not lost when a vessel is broken. Remember when we looked at the properties of clay in lesson one? The grog that is added to saggy, plastic clay for strength is made from pulverized potsherds, pieces of broken pottery. As a nation, as a church, and as individuals, a portion of our strength comes from God's recycling of our broken pieces. Nothing is wasted. When we seek to learn the lessons of the ancient past and of our recent past, we are plumbing the depths of our own clay.

We all have broken things in our lives—broken relationships, broken promises, broken dreams. Don't we sometimes feel like shattered pots? Our lives lie in a jumble of Humpty-Dumpty brokenness, like the debris outside the Potsherd Gate. After we realize that we are unable to put ourselves back together on our own, that's when the magic happens. The Potter scoops up those broken pieces of our life and pulverizes them, using the grog to strengthen the clay of our new vessel.

The picture of those pieces being ground into grog and added to soft clay to build an even stronger pot is what restoration is all about. How many people endure incredible trials and yet, when they come out on the other side, insist they wouldn't change the experience? They understand they are different, far stronger, with their broken shards incorporated into their new vessel.

The bigger the vessel, the more grog it needs for strength. It begs the question—how many broken pieces go into clay that's strong enough to build a massive vessel?

ather, You are the God of second chances. Help us see that our broken lives—our broken hopes and dreams—can be the stuff that will strengthen our new vessels. Amen.

I AM PATIENT

I AM PATIENT

P

"Perhaps there is only one cardinal sin:
impatience. Because of impatience
we were driven out of Paradise;
because of impatience we cannot return."

W. H. AUDEN, 1907–1973

I AM PATIENT BECAUSE
THE PROCESS TAKES TIME

*"As you know, we consider blessed those who have
persevered. You have heard of Job's perseverance
and have seen what the Lord finally brought about."*

JAMES 5:11

Instant gratification. That's what we crave.

When I first studied dollmaking some twenty-five years ago, I was a young, impatient artist. My octogenarian teacher, Mrs. Hanke, had been making porcelain dolls for nearly half a century and knew there could be no shortcuts. I couldn't believe how time-consuming each process was. First I sculpted the face out of clay. Then I learned to make a multipart plaster mold of the clay sculpt, one plane at a time. When the entire mold was done and the clay sculpt removed, the mold had to cure. Only then could wax be poured into the damp mold. Once the wax cooled it was removed, and I sculpted details and deepened the contours with heated tools. Then the whole plaster mold process had to be repeated. Again the molds cured before porcelain-slip casting could begin. The cast parts had to dry. More detailing. Firing. Sanding. Painting. Firing. It was an endless process to create one finished head. And then the process started all over again for each body part.

For some reason I stuck with it. I loved it. I've repeated the painstaking process for close to three hundred different editions over the years, resulting in more than 75,000 handmade dolls. The process itself blessed me with a growing sense of patience. Since there was no way to hurry it up, I learned to slow down and let the process move naturally.

It's much like the task of the potter preparing the clay—that process cannot be hurried either. Back in the workshop, the potter prepares his raw clay. He picks out any foreign particles, tiny pieces of gravel or tree roots and adds water to make the clay into a slip. He passes this slip through a sieve to remove impurities. If one piece of foreign matter is left in the clay or one

REFLECTIONS

"If there is no struggle, there is no progress. Those who profess to favor freedom, and deprecate agitation, are men who want crops without plowing up the ground; they want rain without thunder and lightning."

FREDERICK DOUGLASS
1818–1895

bubble is allowed to remain, all the work that follows is lost. It then dries to a workable plastic consistency.

Before clay is ready for the potter's wheel, it must be wedged. The potter throws the gooey clay onto a porous stone slab or a canvas-covered surface. He scrapes up the mass and slams it onto the slab over and over. This makes the clay pliable with an elastic consistency, removing any pockets that would cause an explosion in the kiln. He finishes by using the heels of his hands to knead the clay.

This preparation process can be monotonous—especially if one is identifying with the clay—but consider the divine Potter. Unlike the earthly potter, He could simply speak the words and transform the clay in an instant.

As a parent, I know the importance of letting my children learn by doing. How many times, on seeing clumsy fingers fumbling at a task, did I itch to step in and finish the task myself? I bit my tongue more than once to keep from saying, "Here, let me do it." It took far more time and involvement to allow them to do it alone, but I would have hobbled them by interfering.

In the book *The Spirit of Clay* by Robert Piepenburg, the author says this about the process: "The other function of wedging, one that many potters feel to be of equal importance, is the unspoken dialogue that is initiated between the potter and the clay." It's interesting that a modern-day potter would phrase it that way.

Perhaps that unspoken dialogue between the Potter and the clay remains the most important element of preparation. As we are thrown against the stone, kneaded, pushed, and pulled, can it really be a form of communication? As clay, our part of the conversation might be "Why me? Why does it have to hurt? Can't this be easier? What have I done?"

If the Potter answered those questions would He say, "It must be done or you'll explode in the kiln"? Or perhaps He'd encourage us to take the long view, saying, "Just wait till you see what you will become."

And although the preparation of the clay requires prolonged hands-on interaction between Potter and clay, it's telling that the harsh effort benefits the clay. After all, it's not the Potter's hands that require a workout.

We wish we could devise a way to make it all go faster, but the Potter knows that good preparation takes time. Besides, we need time to get used to a change. Sometimes it seems to us as if our clay's been on the slab forever.

In my own spiritual walk, this is where I often get edgy. It takes patience to endure the seemingly tedious preparation, but I usually want to sprint to the finish. Unless I allow the Potter to pluck out every extraneous thing, I'll burst when exposed to the fire. This preparation process is not just tedious—sometimes it's torturous. I need to be reminded that before I can anticipate transformation, I may have to be repeatedly slammed against the rock. When I focus on the unspoken communication between the Potter and the clay, it makes the long process of preparation easier to endure.

ather, with the image of clay being slammed to the table, we sometimes find it frightening to contemplate the steps needed to create a strong vessel. Take away our fear and give us patience to endure. Amen.

I AM BEAUTIFUL

I AM BEAUTIFUL

B

"I love the lonely creative hours with God."

Madame Guyon, 1648–1717

I AM BEAUTIFUL BECAUSE
I RESEMBLE MY FATHER

"Then God said, 'Let us make man
in our image, in our likeness.'"

GENESIS 1:26

I 'm often told that the dolls I create resemble me. Though I can't see it in my own sculpting, I recognize this phenomenon in the work of other artists. We seem to bestow something of ourselves to each creation. It's one of the reasons an artist's work can be identified even without a signature.

The work of potters is much the same. Each develops a recognizable style that reflects the artist. Every year I go to a gallery in Charlevoix, Michigan to buy one piece of a favorite potter's work. Although I had never met the potter, I felt as if I knew him through his work. While visiting Sauder Village, a living history museum in Ohio, I stepped into the pottery shed and immediately recognized the work of my potter. That was his working studio, but I knew it by his creations even before I made the connection.

Just think, if the distinctiveness of a clay pot allows us to recognize the potter, how much more wonderful is it when the Potter actually creates in His own image a self-portrait, so to speak?

It's like creation. All the elements of creation were simply called into being: "Let there be . . ." When it came to the creation of man, however, the Trinity honored us by making us in the very image of God.

When Jeremiah's potter finished preparing the clay, he placed a lump of it on the wheel and slowly began to rotate the stone foot wheel, which turned the throwing wheel. His hands circled the clay, lifting it into a shape against gravity. The rotation of the wheel and the expertise of his hands created a symmetry of form.

REFLECTIONS

"Have you ever watched a blacksmith? Did you notice how as he held the iron in the fire it became more and more glowing the longer it lay in the forge, until at last it looked quite like fire? The iron was in the fire, and the fire was in the iron, but the iron was not on fire, nor the fire the iron. When the iron began to glow, the blacksmith could bend it into any shape he desired, but it still remained iron. Even so, we still retain our personality when we allow ourselves to be penetrated by Christ."

SADU SUNDAR SINGH, 1889–1933

Throwing a pot, which is what we call this, is an impossible task for an amateur. The tiniest variation in pressure will cause the pot to careen off center. Jeremiah must have watched for a long time, trying to glean every grain of meaning from the metaphor God gave him.

The very act of creation fascinates us. It's not just our interest in the craft of the artist; as the created, we long to be creative, to follow in our Father's footsteps. For me, the act of sculpting connects me to the work of the Creator.

Sometimes I get lost in the process. The shadows change on the rough wax sculpt as I rotate it to gauge the depth of the features. I slip the electric knife back into the waxer and think about the child's face emerging from the wax. "Lord," I pray, "help me capture a fraction of Your image—let me infuse this face with a piece of the heaven You've planted into each tiny child."

Before I finish praying, I feel that familiar conflict. What am I thinking? Asking God to help me create a doll? I wouldn't be so squeamish about my creations if they were the useful vessels of Jeremiah's potter. But dolls?

One morning during Bible study, I read the passage in Matthew of the woman who poured expensive perfume over Christ's head as He reclined at Simon the Leper's table. The indignant disciples questioned the extravagant gift. "Why this waste?" they asked. "This perfume could have been sold at a high price and the money given to the poor" (Matthew 26:8–9).

I understand that concern. How many times have I voiced the same worry about the dolls? This time the Lord's words to His disciples speak to me: "Why are you bothering this woman? She has done a beautiful thing to me. The poor you will always have with you, but you will not always have me" (Matthew 26:10–11). I know the high value God places on caring for the poor. Is He saying that honoring Him with our best is an even higher priority? Can I honor Him with my gift as well?

God Himself took intense satisfaction in His creation. I can almost picture Him, standing back and surveying each marvel, declaring, "It is good." In Ecclesiastes 5:18–19, Solomon says that we know success and happiness when we find satisfaction in our work. I'm learning to do my best and then step back and say, "It is good." And it is good that the Potter's work in us is ongoing. He restores the no-longer-perfect creation.

There's beauty in the act of throwing a pot. That's not to say that the process of forming the vessel will be easy. It can be tortuous. After all, it requires a constant pressure from the hands of the Potter. We understand why from watching the process, but we still find ourselves chafing at the unrelenting tension in our lives. As Jeremiah observed, when the Potter is ready to open up the lump of clay, His thumbs dig deeply. Without movement and pressure, we remain shapeless lumps of clay.

But there's an intrinsic beauty in the thing joyously created. As the Potter centers us on the wheel, digs His thumbs into our very souls, and begins to pull us off the wheel, we need to focus on the vessel being formed and say with the Potter, "It is good."

 ord, center us on Your wheel.
Dig deep into our clay. We know
without pressure we'll remain shapeless
lumps of clay. Thank You for making us in
Your image. We long to be vessels of beauty.
Amen.

I AM HOPEFUL

I AM HOPEFUL

"Comfort and prosperity have never
enriched the world as much as adversity has.
Out of pain and problems have come the
sweetest songs, and the most gripping stories."

BILLY GRAHAM

I AM HOPEFUL BECAUSE GOD HOLDS MY FUTURE

"For I know the plans I have for you," declares the LORD,
"plans to prosper you and not to harm you,
plans to give you hope and a future."

JEREMIAH 29:11

The potter may squash the clay many times during the creative process. Sometimes the potential vessel comes up an inch or two before a flaw develops and the potter presses it back to the wheel. Other times he will draw it all the way up to a lip, and seeing a wobble, take it back down. The wheel continues to rotate throughout the up-and-down process, until the pot is complete.

Once again, we recognize our spiritual journey in this process. How often do we begin to rise off the wheel, only to be thumped back down? The Potter is in control, and the rising and lowering of the clay is part of the process.

The cycle of up and down reminds me of a long-ago battle in my own life.

Within the first year of our marriage we were delighted to find out we were expecting. Halfway through the pregnancy, however, labor started and we lost a tiny daughter. As we mourned, I agonized over where God was in all this. It felt as if the clay vessel

of my life had been smashed against the wheel.

In spite of our loss, my husband, Keith, and I were anxious to begin our family. Month after month we went through a cycle of hope and despair as the years ticked by and I couldn't conceive. We felt as if the Potter raised us up, only to press us back down. It is hard for anyone who has not experienced infertility to understand the torture—many call it baby-hunger. In the early years when we revealed our struggle, well-meaning friends would try to encourage us, "Two years is not so long." Then, "Three years is not so long." Then . . .

How could they understand what it meant to have our hopes raised and then dashed dozens of times?

REFLECTIONS

"Even in the deepest sinking there is the hidden purpose of an ultimate rising. Thus it is for all men, from none is the source of light withheld unless he, himself, withdraws from it. Therefore, the most important thing is not to despair."

HASIDIC SAYING

Friends from our church seemed to understand best. They knew how intensely we wanted children, and they prayed for us. When we tried adoption, they shared our disappointment at learning there were no infants available. Thumped back down. And they were the ones who celebrated when we discovered that I was finally pregnant again after more than five years.

Halfway into that second pregnancy, I experienced problems. The doctor ordered complete bed rest. Our family and church friends helped with meals and prayed for the safety of the baby. I spent each day flat on my back, alternating between praying and worrying. Seven months into the pregnancy, I went into labor. When I came out of anesthesia from the cesarean delivery, I was told our son only lived three hours.

In the numbing desolation of the weeks that followed, I repeated a long-remembered Bible verse: "When you pass through the waters, I will be with you; and when you pass through the rivers, they will not sweep over you. When you walk through the fire, you will not be burned; the flames will not set you ablaze. For I am the LORD, your God, the Holy One . . . your Savior" (Isaiah 43:2–3). I gave up trying to understand the Potter, yet His presence seemed almost palpable.

When we rejoined our church friends, they bathed us in tears and prayers. One friend prayed boldly, asking God to give us a baby—somehow, anyhow—just give us a baby. We loved him for his simple faith but explained the impossibility of that request. We'd already been through myriad adoption inquiries, and there just weren't any babies. We were tired of the process, and we wanted off the Potter's wheel altogether.

The following Wednesday my doctor called. Without preamble he said, "Don't ask me why I am doing this—I don't like getting involved in private adoption . . . but have your attorney call me within the next ten minutes. I have a beautiful baby waiting for you at the hospital."

A seven-pound baby girl? And we could pick her up at the hospital on Friday? The rest of that day was a blur. By evening, we were shopping for the long-dreamed-of baby furniture.

When we brought Rebecca home from the hospital, no baby was ever more enthusiastically welcomed into a home and community. Now more than twenty-five years later, we can see the vessel the Potter was creating. Sometimes it's only when we can view the Potter's work through the perspective of time that we understand the pattern of those ups and downs.

L ord, too often the process is one of cycles—hope and despair.

Rising up and getting thumped back down.

When we feel caught in what seems like a

never-ending cycle, give us the vision of

eventual transformation and the faith to

trust Your plans. Amen.

I Am Expectant

I AM EXPECTANT

E

"The Lord Jesus is looking about everywhere for that Christian who will remain faithful and loving even when He has withdrawn Himself. If the Lord finds such a faithful soul, when He does return, He rewards the faithfulness of His child. He pours out upon that faithful one abundant goodness and tender caresses of love. Here then is something you must understand. You will have times of spiritual dryness. It is part of the Lord's way."

MADAME GUYON, 1648–1717

I Am Expectant Because Dry Times Yield Growth

"I called him, but he gave me no answer."

SONG OF SOLOMON 5:6 KJV

We spend much of our lives waiting. We wait in lines to buy food. We wait on a street corner for a bus. When we are children, we wait impatiently to grow up. As adults we wait with dread for old age to set in. Some of us wait for healing. Others wait for circumstances to change.

When we read the word *wait* in the Bible, it often means an entirely different thing. In our everyday lives, drumming fingers, twiddling thumbs, or restless pacing usually accompany our waiting. The waiting we see in the Bible is all about supplication and relationship.

When we hear "wait on the Lord," the injunction is to be quiet, to listen, to pray, to anticipate. It's the opposite of the everyday uneasy wait. It's not about lines and delays; it's about being still and getting connected.

We can learn to wait on the Lord in the everyday bustle of life. As we spend precious minutes delayed at the airport or waiting for someone at the doctor's office, we can learn to really wait, to listen for God's voice.

Back in Jerusalem, had Jeremiah seen the pot through to completion, he might have been dismayed to discover that even a perfectly formed vessel still has a long way to go. After the pot is made, the potter turns his back on the vessel while it's put on a shelf to air-dry.

It's an image to ponder—the vessel, set aside, becoming drier and drier. The image resonates with me. It parallels those times when I experience spiritual and emotional dryness. I've noticed that I begin to describe those strange wilderness times with phrases that begin with "I feel . . ." or "I think . . ." For instance, I may *feel* God is far away. Or I *think* He's turned His back on me for some reason. I *feel* as if I can't pray. I *think* God no longer listens.

Imagine the feelings of that set-aside pot, banished to the drying shelf while he hears the potter working on a new vessel. Perhaps he longs to have the potter's hands on his moist clay once again. Instead, he feels his clay body getting drier and drier. What he wouldn't give for

*"There is spiritual and
emotional wilderness.
The mature know
that when they seem
disconnected, the only
sustaining experience is
worship. When they
emerge from the
wilderness, they are
wide-eyed at what God
has accomplished while
they wandered. When
God seems most absent
from us, it is likely he is
keeping us out of the
way of his*

(CONTINUED ON NEXT PAGE)

the potter to simply turn around and acknowledge him. The sun comes in through the window behind him, and with way too much time on his hands, he starts noticing the shadows cast against the shed wall. How come he never noticed relative size before? Some might even characterize him as a modest-sized pot compared to the others. What if his mission in life is to be equally modest?

He looks around, trying to compare his shape to the shape of the other pots in the drying room when he catches a movement through the doorway. It's a new pot rising from the potter's wheel. What? It's the biggest pot yet.

Surely it will hold enough wine for a wedding feast. He feels further diminished, and still the potter never turns away from the moving wheel.

Think . . . Feel . . . the words themselves give a clue to the problem. This set-aside time in our spiritual journey is often marked by words of emotion. The anthropomorphic pot in our example gave in to insecurities and started comparing himself to others. The more diminished he felt, the more his neediness grew. We've all experienced this.

Sometimes insecurity is followed by other emotions like anger. "What am I? Why not

(CONTINUED FROM PAGE 80)

accomplishing what he intends. We can learn to relax a bit in these seeming absences and anticipate some very interesting experiences when they are over. Paul got stuck in Asia Minor thinking he ought to be on his way to Rome. To fill his time he wrote most of Romans. What a time filler. When he got to Rome he found a church that already knew what he was thinking and was likely not confused by his rambling discourses."

LLOYD AHLEM

me?" Or jealousy. "Why does God prosper that person's business when I've been serving Him for twenty years?" or "Why is his ministry skyrocketing when I'm still leading a church of fifty-three grumbling members?" Or it may even take a self-deprecating turn. "I'm worthless and this proves it."

The most important thing to remember is that emotions are great deceivers. Do not trust them.

Our pot didn't have all the facts. The potter knew that if the clay body of the vessel didn't dry completely problems would occur in the firing and the pot could be 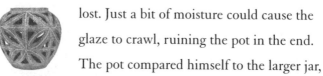 lost. Just a bit of moisture could cause the glaze to crawl, ruining the pot in the end. The pot compared himself to the larger jar, but he had no idea what the potter had in store for him. What if the modest pot were to be decorated with a design of cobalt and gold and become a vessel to hold frankincense for a king? Or what if he remained a modest clay vessel whose only task was to pour drops of water onto lips of children dying from thirst? Who can begin to know the eternal worth of our mission?

In the midst of a dry season in our life, we need to hold on to God's words. Did He say He'd never leave us? Grab that promise. Replace untrustworthy emotions with solid truth. Whether we *feel* like it or not, we need to devour His Word. We still may not *feel* connected, but we've made the intellectual decision to believe His promises.

Hosea 6:3 says, "Let us acknowledge the LORD; let us press on to acknowledge him. As surely as the sun rises, he will appear; he will come to us like the winter rains, like the spring rains that water the earth."

That's a promise, no matter how dry we *feel*.

 ather, there are times of spiritual dryness in our lives. We become parched and long to be drenched with living water once again. When we no longer feel You near, teach us to wait on You and offer a sacrifice of praise to You. Amen.

I AM CONTENT

I AM CONTENT

"The best and most beautiful things
in the world cannot be seen,
nor touched . . . but are felt in the heart."

HELEN KELLER, 1880–1968

I AM CONTENT BECAUSE
OF THE PROMISED OUTCOME

"For now we see through a glass, darkly;
but then face to face: now I know in part;
but then shall I know even as also I am known."

1 CORINTHIANS 13:12 KJV

Schoolchildren often come to our workshops to see how dolls are made. As they walk through the process, they watch our greenware craftsmen working on powdery white porcelain pieces. Without fail, a child will glance over at the flesh-colored doll parts and ask, "How do you get the color on it?"

"The pigment is already in there," I tell them. "You just can't see it."

That always elicits a long discussion. The children think I haven't understood their question. I tell them that the color doesn't develop until the piece is fired. We always walk *en masse* over to the kilns, and I show them the kiln that is being loaded with that day's completed parts—still white. I then show them a kiln with fired parts—flesh-toned. Some pieces have fired to a peachy Caucasian flesh, some to a golden Asian tone, others to a rich African American flesh color. Questions fly again, and they have to go back and look at the greenware once more.

That's like the ceramic process we've been examining. When the pot is completely dry, the potter coats it with a glaze (another clay made of the finest sand and silica mixed with a flux and soda). This unfired glaze is dull and looks like thin, watery clay. Anyone watching this process will wonder why the potter would choose such an ugly coating for his vessel.

As an impatient observer, the work of our Creator often mystifies us—we expected a luminous miracle, and we're disappointed in the dull reality. We still have no idea that it will take an ordeal by fire to see the fulfillment of the Potter's original plan.

REFLECTIONS

"If the doors of perception were cleansed, everything would appear to man as it is, infinite."

WILLIAM BLAKE
1757–1827

It's just like our lives. My friends Norman and Martha Dwight recently retired from a lifetime of service on the mission field. Norman grew up in China, but while on furlough when he was eleven, his family learned they could not return to China because of impending war.

He never had the opportunity to say good-bye to his Chinese friends or his childhood home. What about the years they spent in China? Would all that work be swept away before they ever saw the finished vessel the Potter was forming?

After World War II, China was closed to missionaries. Norman and his bride, Martha, joined his father serving on the mission field in Taiwan. In all the years in Taiwan they heard nothing of the orphaned work in China. In 1979 when the United States recognized Communist China, the door to China creaked open.

At the first opportunity, Norman returned to China to visit their former mission field, now called Xiang-fan. Because of the political climate he proceeded cautiously and asked few questions, fearing possible harm to the Chinese Christians. As he quietly poked around, he could find no trace of the living church they had left fifty years before.

A few years later, Norman led a small group to Xiang-fan. On a solitary evening walk through the town, he discovered a tiny brick building with the words *Gospel Hall* written in Chinese. An elderly gatekeeper led them inside to speak to the young associate pastor. As Norman explained in Chinese who he was, the gatekeeper seemed agitated and drew near. "Norman?" the man asked in English.

The gatekeeper had been a playmate of Norman's nearly half a century before. They talked for hours, sharing stories about the goodness of God. He told Norman about the Chinese Christians who had remained faithful. He refused to dwell on the trials the church had endured over the years but focused instead on the sustaining grace of God.

With full hearts, Norman's group attended a prayer meeting at the little church. Its senior pastor had been one of his father's seminary students. As they said good-bye on their final day in Xiang-fan, Pastor Chang went to the old organ. He bid them farewell with their favorite hymn from more than fifty years before, "God Be with You Till We Meet Again."

The once-dull coating on the vessel of the Chinese church underwent a transformation in Norman's absence. Despite the best attempts by principalities and powers to obliterate the church, their years in the fire created a vessel gleaming with the depth of a burnished finish.

It takes real faith to accept what we cannot see. The Bible tells us, "Now faith is the substance of things hoped for, the evidence of things not seen" (Hebrew 11:1 KJV). Or as the NIV puts it, "being sure of what we hope for and certain of what we do not see."

ord, how we hate it when we can't see what is to come.

We know we need to trust Your promises,

but sometimes we are so faithless and

nearsighted. Forgive and help us. Amen.

I Am Prudent

I AM PRUDENT

P

"The gem cannot be polished without friction,
nor man perfected without trials."

CHINESE PROVERB

I AM PRUDENT BECAUSE IMPETUOUSNESS CAUSES MELTDOWNS

*"So, if you think you are standing firm,
be careful that you don't fall!"*

1 CORINTHIANS 10:12

When the glaze is fully dry, the pot is ready to go into the kiln. If someone were to take that seemingly sturdy sun-dried vessel and fill it with water, the pot would melt into nothing more than a lumpy mass of clay again. The potter can reconstitute his clay at any point until it is fired (vitrified).

That sun-dried pot is like me. How often have I argued with the Lord that I'm ready to hold water, only to melt into mud at the first filling? He knows I've not spent enough time in the fire. It's a striking picture of God's patient love—a love that will reshape the lump of clay over and over again.

Don't you think of Peter when you picture the over-eager pot trying to skip a few steps to get right to the filling?

During the height of Jesus' ministry, after the last bit of bread and fishes had been gathered from the miraculous feeding, Jesus finally escaped the crowds.

He'd sent His disciples into their boat to row across the lake. He needed time to walk up to the mountaintop to pray. It was late when He finished His time of prayer. Looking out across the lake, He could see that the boat had made little progress due to fierce headwinds.

Sometime between three and six in the morning, while the disciples kept busy fighting to keep their fishing boat from capsizing in the storm, Jesus stepped out on the lake and walked across the water toward them. Spume and spray probably engulfed Him until He was close enough to catch their attention. At first the

REFLECTIONS

"Few souls understand what God would accomplish in them if they were to abandon themselves unreservedly to Him and if they were to allow His grace to mold them accordingly."

IGNATIUS
50–107

men panicked, thinking Him a ghost, but once they recognized Him, Peter called out, "Lord, if it's you, tell me to come to you on the water" (Matthew 14:28).

Jesus answered with one word. "Come."

Peter jumped out of the boat and started to walk across the heaving water toward Jesus. When he felt the whip of the wind, he panicked and began to sink. Immediately Christ held out His hand and rescued impetuous, faith-challenged Peter.

It begs the question . . . if Peter had the faith to jump out of the boat into the churning water, what

caused him to shrink halfway through? Some ancient writers like Hilary of Poitiers saw this as a foreshadowing of Peter's eventual weakness and denial at the time of the crucifixion. Who knows? But we recognize the doubt. How many times have we taken on a task only to shrink back at our own weaknesses?

As we look at the fragility of sun-dried vessels, Peter's story reminds us that he was not yet finished and ready for service. But we know the end of the story. Peter goes through his own trial by fire, and an amazing vitrification takes place, turning the once-frightened Peter into the solid stone that the Lord foretold.

But even more dangerous than an overeager volunteer who runs ahead of the process is the poser who appears to be a finished vessel, but merely mimics the process. Perhaps no one created as vivid a character sketch of a poser as John Bunyan with his character "Talkative" in *Pilgrim's Progress*.

As Christian and Faithful journey toward the Celestial City, they see a handsome man in the distance—though they note he's not quite as "comely" up close. He tells them his name is Talkative. He walks alongside Faithful and offers to engage in conversation on any topic. As Faithful converses with the man, the depth of Talkative's knowledge impresses him—he seems to know everything, even about complicated theological subjects.

Faithful moves ahead to tell Christian of this interesting fellow.

Christian merely smiles.

When Faithful questions him further, Christian reveals that he knows Talkative well. Christian points out to Faithful that there's a serious disconnection in the man—that saying and doing are two different things. Here's what Christian says:

> *They are two things indeed, and are as diverse as are the soul and the body; for, as the body without the soul is but a dead carcass, so saying, if it be alone, is but a dead carcass also. The soul of religion is the practical part. . . . [Talkative] thinks that hearing and saying will make a good Christian; and thus he deceiveth his own soul. Hearing is but as the sowing*

of the seed; talking is not sufficient to prove that fruit is indeed in the heart and life. And let us assure ourselves, that at the day of doom men shall be judged according to their fruits.

Nearly four hundred years ago, Bunyan understood that there was more to a vessel than appearances. So whether we've eagerly jumped ahead of the process like the apostle Peter, or whether we thought we could skip the pain and preparation altogether to simply pose as a student of the process like Talkative, we'll still melt into a pile of clay the first time we are put to the test.

L ike Peter, Lord, we sometimes eagerly step out before we're ready. We take our eyes off You and begin to sink like a stone. We're too much like the unfired greenware that looks like a vessel but melts at the first drenching. You love us in spite of our impetuousness. Thank You. When we're like Talkative—trying to fake our way—stop us in our tracks. Save us, O Lord. Amen.

I AM WAITING

W

Consummation

One spark,
inscrutable spark,
in the damp reaches of my soul
trembles,
caught in a whisper
of Spirit wind. Ignite the whole
furnace with flame,
cleansing flame,
'til all that's left, O Lord, is You.

MARLENE CHASE

I Am Waiting Because
God Promises Transformation

"All the days of my hard service I will
wait for my renewal to come."

JOB 14:14

O ne of the wonders of a tour through our workshops is seeing a comparison of before-and-after firing. I always show an unfired porcelain piece next to a fired piece. Not only has the pigment developed in the kiln, but the fired piece is also visibly smaller than the greenware piece. With the porcelain we use, the shrinkage is a striking 17 percent. During the time in the kiln, all impurities are burned away. It's a remarkable metaphor.

To vitrify the earthenware pots thrown by Jerusalem potters, it had to fire at a temperature of about two thousand degrees Fahrenheit. This firing process is comparable to the crucible for metals. When the impurities burn away, just like our porcelain doll pieces, the vessel is visibly smaller when removed from the kiln. What's remarkable is that the exact shape is still intact right down to the fingerprint marks of the potter. This is the transformation. Firing causes a change in the chemical properties of the clay. No longer porous, it now holds water indefinitely. It is more akin to stone than to earth.

With human vessels, transformation usually occurs slowly; and we don't see a single point of vitrification, as with our metaphor. I did see it happen, though, in the life of one young woman from my Sunday school class. After graduation from high school, Amelia Eck and her sister Daphne made plans to take a short-term mission trip to India to serve in one of Mother Teresa's charity homes for the dying and destitute.

The experience changed Amelia forever. She wrote a long letter about her experiences. She told of sitting by the bedside of a dying woman and being able to do nothing more than shoo flies

REFLECTIONS

"What fire is this that warms my soul? What light is this that so brightens my soul? O fire that burns forever, and never dies, kindle me! O light which shines eternally, and never darkens, illuminate me! O that I had my heat from you, most Holy fire! How sweetly do you burn!"

AUGUSTINE, 354–430

out of her open mouth with a limp hankie; of temperatures so hot the girls stuck to velour van seats soaked with the sweat of hundreds of previous riders; of pressing crowds; of day workers sleeping on bare paths leading up to their rooms; and of the constant cacophony of voices and horns and animals and children. Amelia wrote:

"One day I went to work at *Shishu Bhavan*, a children's home. I followed Sister Bethany into a room of attention-starved kids and noticed a boy in the middle of the room. He lay facedown on the cement floor, squirming and moaning. At first I thought he was mentally retarded, but when I picked him up I could see he was blind. He had one eye missing that was squinted shut. The other eye was glazed white. I tried to hold him in my lap, but he was so restless he squirmed out. I laid him on the floor beside me and petted his face and tummy until he stopped crying.

"I stood him up beside me and began talking and laughing with him. I put his hands on my face, letting him feel the balls of my smiling cheeks. He was curiously fascinated. Then I took his other hand and put it on my eye, which I squinted shut like his. That was when I saw his first smile. We sat and 'talked' and laughed together until it was time to leave."

"This incident didn't mean as much to me until I came home. I read 1 Corinthians 9:22–23, 'I have become all things to all men so that by all possible means I might save some. I do all this for the sake of the gospel, that I may share in its blessings.' This little boy didn't connect with me until he felt my eye that he thought was just like his."

A short-term mission trip to a third-world-country often changes someone's perspective, but Amelia's trip took place close to ten years ago, and she's never been the same. Some would say she decreased her options. With fashion magazine–type beauty and honor-student grades, most would think Amelia had a whole world of opportunities open to her.

That decrease reminds us of clay—it shrinks after all the impurities are fired away. It's another picture of transformation. "He must increase, but I must decrease" (John 3:30 KJV).

Amelia ended her letter with, "When we do what God desires, we are so richly blessed. When we do what we desire, we mess things up; and not just for ourselves but for others too. I want to live my life, holy and pleasing to the Lord, as if each day is my last."

And she does. Amelia Eck continues to serves the Lord in a radical way, working full-time at Westside Ministries, a Christian urban youth organization. She meets the definition of *transformed*—she holds living water, bears the fingerprints of the Potter, and is more akin to stone than earth.

F ather, we thank You for giving us the image of the Potter and the clay. We understand that the whole process leads up to the kiln. It's all about purification. Sometimes we are afraid to seek spiritual purity because we know that every impurity must be fired out. Give us the courage to seek it. Amen.

I AM EXCITED

E

"The most perfect way of seeking God, and the most suitable order, is not for us to attempt with bold curiosity to penetrate to the investigation of His essence, which we ought more to adore than meticulously to search out, but for us to contemplate Him in His works, whereby He renders Himself near and familiar to us, and in some manner communicates Himself."

JOHN CALVIN, 1509–1564

I AM EXCITED BECAUSE I WILL REFLECT THE FACE OF THE POTTER

"Seek the LORD, and his strength:
seek his face evermore."

PSALM 105:4 KJV

Pottery, as well as my own porcelain work, is unique in art media. The decoration, whether china paint or glaze, is not painted on and allowed to dry as in oil paintings or watercolor. The china paint we use on porcelain stays forever wet until it goes back into the kiln and is fired into the piece. The glaze or china paint actually becomes a part of the clay body. It's impervious to wear. That's why so many ancient pottery pieces remain with us today.

The process is fascinating. As Jeremiah visited the potter, he might have noticed the chalky glaze on the pieces waiting to be fired. Perhaps he also watched the potter unloading his kiln and saw the miraculous change from chalky glaze to vivid color. The intense heat of the kiln caused the dull clay coating to undergo a metamorphosis. Where there was no indication of color before firing, now the vessel was clothed in brilliant color, often with a glasslike (china) finish or a satin (bisque) finish. Watching the transformation of an earthenware vessel to an objet d'art is an epiphany, a flash of the Divine.

When I consider the parallel to my own spiritual walk, it's a picture worth contemplating. Just think: That dull coat of unfired glaze that's reflected in our mirrors each day may someday emerge from the fire a crystalline color—a color so pure and translucent that others will see the Potter's face reflected in the surface.

According to the Bible, Moses experienced this, but only for a time. His face reflected the face of God when he came down from Mount Sinai. The people saw it immediately, an other-worldly radiance. Moses had to go often to the mount to talk to

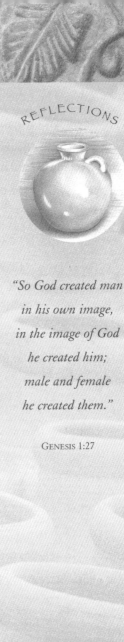

REFLECTIONS

"*So God created man in his own image, in the image of God he created him; male and female he created them.*"

GENESIS 1:27

God and renew this shining reflection. In between times, when the glow started to fade, Moses wore a veil (see 2 Corinthians 3:13).

Many scholars believe this is a picture of the old covenant God made with His people, which had to be constantly renewed. We live under the new covenant, which means we have the presence of the Holy Spirit. According to 2 Corinthians 3:18: "And we, who with unveiled faces all reflect the Lord's glory, are being transformed into His likeness with ever-increasing glory, which comes from the Lord, who is the Spirit."

What a promise. Though I'm pretty sure the complete transformation will not take place this side of eternity, we long to reflect the face of the Potter. With the help of the Holy Spirit, we are being transformed to do just that.

Instead of the instantaneous transformation that takes place in a glazing fire, our metamorphosis is probably more like the patina acquired by an unglazed pot over centuries of handling.

I think back to my own moment of decision, that day in 1957 when I walked to the front of children's church and prayed the sinner's prayer. I may have been only seven, but I remember aching for forgiveness and longing to follow Christ. What I didn't understand then was that I wouldn't be changed immediately. After that service I walked out to the curb where my father sat in our turquoise 1954 Ford station wagon. Did he see the change in me? I don't remember the days that followed, but I undoubtedly fought with my brother and sisters, disobeyed my parents, and continued much as I had before, even though something had changed forever in my life.

Now, nearly a half century later, I recognize what antique dealers know. The more an object is handled, the more beautiful it becomes. The natural oils of our hands lend a rich patina to unglazed pottery. Repetitive handling smoothes the rough edges and gently wears any sharpness off. If the color seemed garish when new, age gentles it to a muted sheen.

So could it be that we're more like an unglazed earthenware vessel than a glossy pot? If someone catches a glimpse of the Potter's face in us, perhaps it's due to His hands on our lives throughout the years. Hopefully as we age and as we grow in Christ, He'll continue to deepen that patina.

Lord, we long for transformation—instantaneous and vibrant. While we believe that change will happen someday, help us recognize gradual transformation as we seek to become a vessel worthy of the Potter. Amen.

I AM USEFUL

I AM USEFUL

"Oh, to be but emptier, lowlier,

Mean, unnoticed, and unknown,

And to God a vessel holier,

Filled with Christ, and Christ alone;

Naught of earth to cloud the glory,

Naught of self the light to dim,

Telling forth the wondrous story,

Emptied—to be filled with Him."

P. G., An Unidentified Brethren Writer

LESSON ELEVEN

I AM USEFUL BECAUSE HE CREATED ME FOR SERVICE

"But now, by dying to what once bound us, we have been released from the law so that we serve in the new way of the Spirit, and not in the old way of the written code."

ROMANS 7:6

bjet d'art or household utensil, the finished vessel was created to be used—perhaps for storing soothing and fragrant oil; for holding nourishing food; or to be filled with clean, clear water.

Usefulness. That's always been one of the reservations about my own art. It's not practical pots I create; it's very expensive, very superfluous porcelain dolls. Too often I've worried about the sheer frivolity of my craft. Instead of the sturdy pot the Jerusalem potter created, my creation is, well, unnecessary. Maybe that's one of the reasons I always loved the parable of the cracked pot. Have you heard it? A water bearer had two large pots, one hung on each end of a pole, which he carried across his neck. One of the pots had a crack in it, while the other pot was perfect and always delivered a full portion of water.

At the end of the long walk from the stream to the master's house, the cracked pot always arrived only half full. For years this went on daily, with the bearer delivering only one and a half pots full of water to his master's house. Of course, the perfect pot was proud of its accomplishments, fulfilled in the design for which it was made. But the poor cracked pot was ashamed of its own imperfection, and miserable that it was unable to accomplish what it had been made to do.

After enduring this bitter shame, the pot spoke to the water bearer one day by the stream. "I am ashamed of myself and I apologize to you."

"Why?" asked the bearer. "What are you ashamed of?"

"I have been able, for these past two years, to deliver only half my load because this crack in my side causes water to leak out all the way back to your master's house. Because of my flaws, you have to do all of this work, and you don't get the full value from your efforts," the pot said.

REFLECTIONS

"Behold, Lord, an empty vessel that needs to be filled. My Lord, fill it. I am weak in faith; strengthen me. My love is cold; warm me and make me fervent in love toward my neighbor."

MARTIN LUTHER
1483–1546

The water bearer felt sorry for the old cracked pot, and in his compassion he said, "As we return to the master's house, I want you to notice the beautiful flowers along the path." Indeed, as they went up the hill, the old cracked pot took notice of the sun warming the beautiful wildflowers on the side of the path, and was cheered somewhat. But at the end of the trail, it still felt the old shame because it had leaked out half its load, and so again the pot apologized to the bearer for its failure.

The bearer said to the pot, "Did you not notice that there were flowers only on your side of the path, and not on the other pot's side? That's because I have always known about your flaw. I planted flower seeds on your side of the path, and every day while we've walked back from the stream, you've watered them. For two years I have been able to pick these beautiful flowers to decorate my master's table. Without you being just the way you are, he would not have this beauty to grace his house."

So dolls may not have the usefulness of Jeremiah's pot, but we are all created to be used for service—some for carrying water, others for spreading beauty.

And each of us has flaws. We're all cracked pots. But if we will allow Him, the Lord will use our flaws to grace His Father's table. In God's great economy, nothing goes to waste. Don't be afraid of your flaws. Acknowledge them, and you, too, can bring something beautiful to the Father.

It's all about service. A friend loaned me the journals of Ann Berg, a missionary in the Congo. She kept a commonplace book throughout her life—rich with stories and testimonies of selfless servants. One of those, whose story was told in an entry from 1961, was Ndowe Albert. According to Ann, he served as a village teacher. Because he had no formal education, he received no pay. But he loved the Lord. She remembers that he built a tiny chapel, and on the mud pulpit, before it dried, he inscribed the words, "Jesus Saves. O Come to Jesus Today."

Ndowe Albert treasured his Bible and took it with him everywhere, including Likimi where he went to visit a relative. He got the proper road documents before he left, but it made no difference to authorities there. They arrested him for holding services in the yard of his neighbor. It gave them the excuse of fining him 130 francs. Since he had no money, he went to jail. They took away his clothes, his songbook, and his Bible. When he was released, they refused to give his belongings back to him. Miss Berg noted how great this loss must have been to him, but all he could talk about were the two other Christians he met in jail and how the three of them had led another prisoner to Jesus.

He understood what matters.

The purpose of transformation is to be fitted for service. It is a process. The vessel exists as a testimony to the Potter, but it is the act of being filled and pouring out that completes the incarnational act of the Potter.

L ord, we ask that You use us for Your service, even as You continue to perfect us as vessels. Let us offer our imperfections to You, knowing that You don't necessarily call those who are already equipped—You equip those You call. Amen.

THE UNCONTAINABLE

The uncontainable

bridges the vaulted dome of sky,

rides the wind from east to west,

cups oceans in His hands.

Who can hold Him—

Master of the Universe, Holy One—

Filling every space?

The uncontainable

allowed Himself to be contained—

The Holy of Holies in a tabernacle box

with manna, stone, and Aaron's rod.

Later a trough

for feeding hungry sheep and cows

carried the Christ of God.

The uncontainable

Lay in a crypt of chiseled stone—

damp and dark and deadly cold

where lizards crawled and mosses crept.

The uncontainable,

Holy of Holies, delights now to dwell

in a humble jar of clay.

MARLENE CHASE

IMPRESSIONS IN CLAY TEAM

ACQUIRING EDITOR
Peg Short

COPY EDITOR
Ali Childers

BACK COVER COPY
Michele Straubel

COVER DESIGN
Paetzold Associates

COVER ART
JoAnn Anderson

INTERIOR DESIGN
Julia Ryan, DesignByJulia
www.designbyjulia.com

PRINTING AND BINDING
Color House Graphics

The typeface for the text of this book is
ElegantGaramondBT

Since 1894, Moody Publishers has been dedicated to equip and motivate people to advance the cause of Christ by publishing evangelical Christian literature and other media for all ages, around the world. Because we are a ministry of the Moody Bible Institute of Chicago, a portion of the proceeds from the sale of this book go to train the next generation of Christian leaders.

If we may serve you in any way in your spiritual journey toward understanding Christ and the Christian life, please contact us at www.moodypublishers.com.

"All Scripture is God-breathed and is useful for teaching, rebuking, correcting and training in righteousness, so that the man of God may be thoroughly equipped for every good work."
—2 TIMOTHY 3:16, 17

MOODY
PUBLISHERS

THE NAME YOU CAN TRUST®